Children and Christian Initiation: A Practical Guide to the Precatechumenate

Kathy Coffey

Living the Good News, Inc.,
a division of The Morehouse Group
in cooperation with
The North American Forum
on the Catechumenate

Contents

Second Printing: 1998

Living the Good News, Inc.
   a division of The Morehouse Group
Editorial Offices: 600 Grant Street, Suite 400
Denver, CO 80203

James R. Creasey, Publisher

Printed in the United States of America
Illustrations: Anne Kosel
Cover Photographs: Mark Kiryluk
Cover Design: Bob Stewart, Bass Creative

ISBN 0-8192-8001-1

Chapter
1

We Hold a Treasure

"As the little prince dropped off to sleep, I took him in my arms and set out walking once more. I felt deeply moved, and stirred. It seemed to me that I was carrying a very fragile treasure. It seemed to me, even, that there was nothing more fragile on all the Earth."

—Antoine de Saint-Exupery, *The Little Prince*

If you are the parent or sponsor of a young person being initiated, or if you serve on the initiation team, you may feel the spirit of *The Little Prince*. The children with whom you will journey are precious and vulnerable. While questions or worries are natural, you want to serve them well.

This guidebook is designed as a resource for catechists, parents, team members, sponsors, godparents and community members who participate in the Christian initiation of children. It will serve as a tool providing helpful background and boosting your confidence in the process you have begun. It will enable you to make a transition from more formal sessions and public rites into informal, one-on-one chats with individual children. If you dread awkward silences, try the activities suggested to facilitate faith sharing and to communicate scripture, customs and tradition. A conversation about the incarnation, which might otherwise seem stilted, can flow easily over the making of a creche. Grace before a meal may seem more natural as the family passes a blessing cup.

This book covers the first phase of the process, the inquiry period or pre-catechumenate. The questions and activities it includes may be adapted for use with children, other team members and sponsors, or private reflection.

What's in it for me?

You may discover, as others have, that your participation in this process not only represents a great service to the child, but also enriches you. Sometimes people who have taken their religious faith for granted or left it "on hold" while they focused on other areas of their lives find a "spark" through the initiation process.

As they support another person, they find old assumptions challenged and long-held beliefs re-invigorated. The faith could be compared to a rusty teapot: in polishing it for another, we discover the shining treasure it is for ourselves. Seeing the Catholic heritage of word, symbol and rite through a child's eyes can lead to a new appreciation of its richness.

What's in it for the child?

Most children never have enough one-on-one time with adults. Some experts would say they never receive enough love. Children today are affected by major changes in every social structure: school, family, church. They long for the security and meaning offered by the God who created them. They want to belong to a community that offers them order and diversity, service and mission. They yearn for the stability and reassurance of a one-on-one relationship with a trusted adult.

The initiation process responds to these deep needs. It introduces children to an infinite source of love: God revealed through Jesus. Hearing the gospel, children learn much about Jesus and fall in love with him. They develop a life-long attitude of prayer, turning to Jesus in continuous communication. Through the initiation process, the community welcomes children warmly and shares with them the finest resources of its tradition. Finally, the process provides children time with a caring adult.

The 1993 National Study of the Changing Workforce found that 66 percent of parents employed outside the home don't have enough time with their children. What might the statistic be if children were asked? They often find their parents tired, overextended and at times, cranky. When can they talk to them about the things that really count, or ask their most troubling questions?

Parents will attest that children's profound questions arise at the most inopportune times: in the midst of a traffic jam, when something in the oven smells funny or when they are preoccupied with another problem. At that moment, the child asks the zinger: "Why do you believe in God?" or "Why do we have to die?"

While the "inopportunity principle" still applies to initiation, at least the process creates times and spaces in busy schedules for exploring the big issues. During this inquiry period, there are many opportunities for adults and children to meet socially, to ask questions, to tell stories and "break open the word" or explore the scripture. Different prayers and rituals are celebrated together. Meetings can be held in homes as well as at the parish. The emphasis is not on classroom learning, but on what children absorb from the people around them and the rites they celebrate. The challenge to the adult is to continue the discussions begun in the sessions and to reflect on the rites during private times with the child.

Even if you are a parent who has lived closely with this child for many years, this process offers a new way of relating. For most parents, conversations with their children revolve around "What's for dinner?" "Have you done your homework?" and "What time should I pick you up?" The initiation process plunges participants into deeper waters. "Who am I?" "Who is God?" "Where do I find God?" are typical of the questions that may emerge.

As you confront the big questions, don't worry that you need a Ph.D. in Theology or must have all the answers. Some of the questions that children raise have perplexed the finest minds in human history. Look at the first disciples. Jesus started out with pretty ordinary people: fishermen and housewives, tax collectors and women drawing water at the well. If he could work through them, he can work through us.

Nor do you need to worry about knowing doctrines or memorizing rules and prayers. The process of initiation is more like going steady than like going to school. While knowledge is an important dimension, faith is "caught" more than "taught." Many people who memorized the *Baltimore Catechism* came away from it malnourished, unconvinced that Jesus loved them personally. The hope for initiation is that the child will become so closely bonded with Jesus, with friends in the Christian community and with the gospel way of life, that the union will last a lifetime. In that long span, there will be plenty of time to learn intellectual content.

Chats with Children

Pause now to list the chances you could create to be alone with the child being initiated. A few opportunities are given as starters:
- cocoa and donuts after Mass
- bedtime
- a long walk
- an ice cream cone together
- the drive home after an initiation session
- a fishing trip or playground visit
- taking a tour of the church
- other

Remember saving a corsage after a dance, or collecting souvenirs on a vacation? It seems a basic human instinct to gather reminders of special times. Initiation is no different. Both you and the child will treasure these reminders in years to come. At the outset, think of a way to write down ideas and preserve projects or crafts you or the child create. After the creation has been initially displayed on the bulletin board or refrigerator, where can you save it permanently?
- a scrapbook?
- a journal?
- a special box?
- other

Indeed, "we hold a treasure," both in our children and in the church to which we welcome them. To serve as a channel between the two is a rare opportunity, a blessing.

Chapter

2

Overview of Initiation

In *The Heart of the Hunter*, Laurens van der Post describes a woman in the
Kalahari desert holding her infant up to the stars. She chants in prayer
that he might have the heart of a star, "a hunting heart, that seeks with
courage and finds the nourishment which is needed for life."

Sometimes when we're starting a long trip, hunting or seeking, it's helpful to have a map of where we're going. This chapter maps out the initiation process. Knowing its key components, its organization and its termi-
nology is helpful background before getting started.

The Meaning of Initiation
For children, initiation means bonding with a group, making their own
the customs, values, symbols, stories and celebrations of that group. They
are familiar with a similar process if they have joined the Boy Scouts or
Girl Scouts, 4H Club or a baseball team.

What makes this process unique is getting to know Jesus and falling in
love with him. Responding to the gospel stories, children begin a dynam-
ic that will continue throughout their lives. To grow closer to Christ, they
join his body on earth, the church's life of prayer and service.

Key Components
Children
The children who participate in this process are between ages seven and
seventeen. Most of them have not been baptized as infants and are
preparing to celebrate all three sacraments of initiation—baptism, confirmation and eucharist—usually at the Easter Vigil. Some of them have

been baptized in another Christian tradition, or have been baptized in the Catholic Church but not catechized. They are supported by peer companions, other children who are baptized and who are now preparing for the sacraments of confirmation and eucharist. While recognizing that teenagers participate in this process, this book on the precatechumenate follows the usage of the *Rite* (*Rite of Christian Initiation of Adults*, RCIA) by referring to all participants as children. If you are the parent or sponsor of a teenager, your support is just as important as it is for a younger child. This book includes activities and examples for teenagers.

Families

Children seek initiation with the support of their parents or guardians, or on their own with parental permission. This means that the parent is crucial to the child's faith formation. Before a child enters any formalized religious instruction, he or she learns a great deal about God: from the way he or she is cuddled and rocked, fed and diapered.

The parent's voice and touch communicate the image of a compassionate God who cares for a helpless, dependent infant. Whether or not the baby's first cries are answered leads to a lifetime of trust or mistrust. For the other side of the coin is also true: the abused or neglected child carries internal scars throughout a lifetime. While God's grace and healing are boundless, the mark made on a child by a parent, whether for good or ill, is indelible. Psychologists estimate that institutions can exert only 10 percent of the influence parents have in shaping attitudes and values. If the gospel way of life becomes real for the child, it is largely because the parent lives it in the home.

Andrew Greeley's research confirms that parents can bring children to a high "grace scale," that is, a positive attitude toward life as gift. Greeley found no correlation between this attitude and the years spent in formal religious education. Rather, the key element was a relationship with a person who acted as a sacrament of God's presence in the child's life.

In the initiation process, a parent can serve as the child's sponsor but not a child's godparent. If the parent chooses not to be involved in this process, the church appoints a sponsor. The child may also choose a godparent (*RCIA* #307). The sponsor and godparent model for the child a Christ-like way of life.

Community

The concept of community can be seen both in the large sense of the parish and in the context of the family. It is important that children being initiated form relationships with people who embody for them the Christian way of life. Through experiencing these friendships, they learn more about the Christian life than through only studying doctrine. Thus, the Christian community is more important for what it *is* than for what it *does*.

Before the child is ever introduced to a large faith community, he or she learns about community at home: sorting the laundry, buying groceries, choosing the TV channel. Jesus and the first Christians lived a long time ago. To understand how we remember Jesus, children must first know family memories. They should hear the stories of grandma's feud with the landlord, their parents' first date, the day they were born, the day they first met their stepsister. It is difficult to belong to an extended parish family until someone has first belonged to a nuclear family.

Liturgical Catechesis

This phrase combines two things:
- liturgy—the church's public worship, especially eucharist and the sacraments.
- catechesis—the formation and guidance that trains children in the Christian way of life.

Together, the two words mean our faith expressed through our communal rites, symbols, stories and celebrations. Through these, we enter mysteries and deepen our relationship with God.

Liturgical catechesis is vital to initiation because of its power to bring about conversion and transformation. Today children are bombarded by messages from the media selling values that often run counter to Christian ideals. The church's message can come to children in the same way, through imaginative rather than verbal channels. To the child's need for belonging, affirmation and meaning, the church responds with the symbols of God's love. Author Paul Philibert proposes that these symbols can "landscape" the child's inner world.

For an example, consider the child who sings "We Belong to the Family of God," hears the gospel story of Jesus feeding 5,000, exchanges a sign of peace, prays for those in the community who are sick or grieving, and receives the eucharist. Through several senses, this child gets a powerful message about belonging and being fed. Reflecting afterward on that liturgy can expand and deepen the child's understanding.

Children will make their own meaning, and liturgy will not always be perfect. Nevertheless, the *Rite* holds up this vision as normative. So, when we plan a special event like a wedding or party, we hope for an ideal. In reality, someone may get drunk; someone else may come late. Those limitations don't prevent our imagining the ideal.

Prayer
Good communication is essential to any relationship. In our relationship with God, that communication takes the form of prayer. The process of initiation gives children many ways of speaking with and listening to God that can shape a constant attitude. Using both traditional and spontaneous prayer forms, the child becomes a person whose heart and mind are often turned toward God.

Service
Prayer flows into action, and the scriptures form children in an attitude of mission. From breaking open the word each week, children learn the importance of serving others. They see how the Christian people around them take opportunities to act like Christ in their homes, their schools, their parishes and neighborhoods. Just as a young basketball player imitates adult moves on the court, so the young Christian follows the

example others set. While these first actions may seem small, they are not insignificant. They lay the groundwork for a lifetime of mission.

Organization of the Process
Though the initiation process can begin at any time, it is organized around the liturgical year, not the school year or the calendar year.

Because conversion is unique to each individual, there is no set schedule for the process. It is gradual and depends on the needs of the child. The four periods of the process can occur at any time of year, although the third usually coincides with Lent and the fourth with the Easter season. Rites mark the bridges between the periods.

Period 1: Precatechumenate or Inquiry
During this time, the Christian community introduces the child to God in Christ Jesus. Goals of this period are welcoming the child, eliciting his or her concerns and introducing various forms of prayer. The rite of acceptance or welcome marks the end of this period and the beginning of the next.

Period 2: Catechumenate
The goal of this period is to deepen faith. The goal is achieved through exploring the gospel stories, participating in the community's prayer and service, and celebrating minor rites. This period flows into the rite of election.

Period 3: Purification and Enlightenment
This period usually coincides with Lent and is the spiritual preparation for Easter. Its spirit is that of prayerful retreat. Children concentrate on the traditional Lenten practices of prayer, fasting and almsgiving, celebrating at least one scrutiny. This period leads to full sacramental initiation in baptism, confirmation and eucharist.

Period 4: Mystagogy
During this period, the children explore the meaning of the sacraments they have received. They continue to participate in prayer, service and community celebrations. They meet for a full year, until the first anniversary of their initiation.

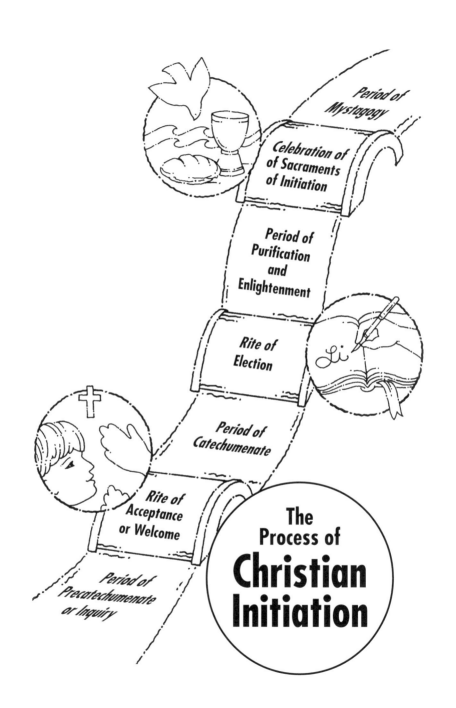

Period of Mystagogy

Celebration of of Sacraments of Initiation

Period of Purification and Enlightenment

Rite of Election

Period of Catechumenate

Rite of Acceptance or Welcome

The Process of **Christian Initiation**

Period of Precatechumenate or Inquiry

A Practical Guide to the Precatechumenate

Background on the Period of Precatechumenate or Inquiry

"If seeds in the black earth can turn into such beautiful roses, what might the human heart become in its long journey to the stars?"
—G.K. Chesterton

The child beginning the process of initiation is starting a long journey, one that will continue throughout a lifetime. While we recognize that this period marks the first step, at the same time we honor the "seeds" that have been sown. God is already present in the child's life, and as Thomas Merton says, even the first stirrings of the desire to please God are pleasing to God.

Much of the evangelization of this period may have already happened outside formal sessions. The role of adults who represent the initiating church is to act like a giant ear, open and receptive to children's doubts and concerns. Sometimes it takes skill to draw out their questions, but these are essential to this stage of the process.

Purposes of This Period
- To become friends (through social activities and informal sharing).
- To explore the ways that Christ is present in peoples' lives.
- To introduce varied forms of prayer, encouraging a life of prayer.

Getting Started
In order to prepare yourself for the journey of initiation with the child, consider the following suggestions:

- Read the *Rite of Christian Initiation of Adults*, especially Part 2 for Children.
- Use the material in chapter 4 of this book for personal reflection, to clarify your own religious belief and practice.
- Reflect on your strengths and those of the team, or other people involved in the process. Think about the particular resources your parish community can offer its children. Complete the sentence, "Wouldn't it be great if we...?"
- Consider how much you know about this child. The material in chapter 5 will help you understand his or her particular learning style. For instance, children who may not seem especially verbal may express themselves more freely through bodily motion (mime or charades), or art. If this is the case, offer opportunities for self-expression other than conversation.
- Consider how much you know about the child's family. Even if this is your own child, you may want to reflect on these questions:
  — What has been the child's or family's experience of church?
  — What is the family constellation? (siblings, stepparents, grandparents, etc.)
  — Which adults in the family are most interested in the initiation process? Why do they support the child's initiation now?
  — What life issues are most pressing for this family?

Preparing for a Session

If possible, find out in advance what issues and scriptures will be discussed.

As you consider the *issue*, ask:
- What has been my experience with this issue?
- What has been this child's experience with it?

As you read the *scripture*, ask:
- What is the good news in this passage for me?
- What is the good news for this child?
- What is the best way to help the child make a link between his or her experience and this reading?
- What one word in the passage strikes me most? Why?
- What does this scripture call me to do? What might it call this child to do? What action can we take together?

For example, let's say that your child attends a session like the one on page 52 in *Children and Christian Initiation: A Practical Guide*. The family issue is sibling problems; the scripture is Luke 15:11-32. The goal of the sessions is to help children see that sibling problems are normal. God can act through these relationships, even the tough ones. Most importantly, Jesus describes God as a merciful father who loves each child despite his flaws.

Following Up the Session

During the session, the children roleplay situations of sibling conflict. If you watch your child participate, you have abundant starters for a conversation afterward:

* You played the role of the brother/sister like an Academy Award winner! How did you know all the right things to say?

If you did not observe, you have a different opportunity. Ask the child:

* Would you tell me about the sibling roleplay?
* Would you have made any changes in it?
* Did you like the way the roleplay ended? Do you think it would have ended that way at your house?
* Who did you like best in the story: the father? the older brother? the younger brother? Which one are you most like?
* How could parents be more like the father in the story? How could you be like the father?
* Do you think God might be like that father? If so, how? If not, why?
* During the prayer service, what places did you name where you would like to act as the merciful father did?

If your child likes art, he or she may want to sculpt the story figures from clay or pipe cleaners, or make some from felt. These can then be used to retell the parable. When you tell the child goodbye or tuck the child into bed that night, be sure to echo the words of the father, perhaps in your own words, using the child's name: "(*Name*), you are always with me, and all that is mine is yours." With the child, you may also want to pray in the words of St. Francis of Assisi:

> Lord, make me an instrument of your peace: where there is hatred, let me sow love; where there is injury, pardon; where there is despair, hope; where there is darkness, light; and where there is sadness, joy.
> O Divine Master, grant that I may not so much seek to be consoled as

to console, to be understood as to understand, to be loved as to love. For it is in giving that we receive, it is in pardoning that we are pardoned, and it is in dying that we are born to eternal life.

Let's take another example. If your child attends the session on bullies in *Children and Christian Initiation: A Practical Guide* (p. 54), prepare by asking yourself:
- What has been my experience with bullies?
- What has been this child's experience with bullies?
- How does Christ show us a different use of power?

The Orphaned Princess

After the session, tell the child Edwina Gateley's story of the orphaned princess:

> When a king and queen knew that foreign invasion was imminent and their family would be killed, they preserved their daughter's life by sending her to live anonymously with a pig farmer. The child grew up unaware of her royal lineage until one day an old woman, who knew the truth, whispered, "You are the daughter of the most high king." After that, the orphaned princess still dug potatoes and fed pigs but with a new dignity, a restored sense of her noble heritage.

Without preaching a word about morality, you can tease out the implications of this story in the weeks ahead. Just as the orphan had royal parents, so we have a royal lineage as children of God, Creator and King of the universe. The fact that we are God's daughters and sons has many implications for daily life.

For example, when Ashley is tempted to bully her annoying little brother, say something along these lines or elicit her thoughts in the matter: "I bet the orphaned princess sometimes wanted to beat up her brother too. But then she remembered that he was an orphaned prince, also far from home. She thought how it would sadden their parents, the king and queen, if they were cruel to each other. So she carried her anger outside and threw rocks in a pond. They made an enormous splash."

Such an approach builds on the positive (we act like royalty because we are redeemed and resurrected by Jesus) rather than the negative (if you lay a finger on your brother, you'll be punished). Positive motivation can influence our behaviors. We act morally because we have so much to be grateful for and celebrate, not because we fear God's wrath.

It gives God the human face of the king and queen, who are sad when we fail to be the best we can be. Finally, it provides a healthy outlet for the anger: the satisfying "thunk" of rocks hitting water, rather than stuffing the anger or thwacking the younger brother.

The story might be used in a totally different way by relating it to God's creation. If Jose admires the light on the water, the trout he's caught or the silhouettes of palm trees, invite him to join you in praise of God the Creator and King. As the mystic Julian of Norwich said, "The fullness of joy is to behold God in everything."

If you are parenting or sponsoring a teenager, you might work on dramatizing the story of the orphaned princess for younger members of the initiation group or for children in the parish nursery or day care center. Create the following props:
• crowns for the king and queen
• pig ears, faces or snouts
• a wig and cane for the old woman
• a shovel and potatoes for the princess

As you work, discuss:
• Why is it important for children to hear this story?
• What message in the story do we want to bring out?
• How do you think it might affect teenagers if they really believed they were royalty?

Chapter
4

Personal Reflection

In the process of Christian initiation, *what* we give the children is not nearly as important as *who* we give them: ourselves. The good news came first in the person of Jesus, not in a book. That continues to be true: the human touch, voice, lap, hug and fragrance give the child his or her first messages about the divine. Think how this has been true in your own life.

Name that Mentor

Name the people who served as models or mentors as your faith developed. Another name for them might be the "uncanonized saints" in your life. Go as far back in memory as you need to. Reflect on or talk about:

- What quality in this person most impressed you?
- Did he or she talk about a faith life or spirituality? Or was the message unspoken?
- What do you remember doing with this person?
- Why do you think your activities together had so much influence?
- What did you learn from this person about how you in turn could companion, parent or sponsor a child?

A Practical Guide to the Precatechumenate

An example comes from *She Who Is* by Elizabeth Johnson. She quotes a Puerto Rican woman named Inez: "But if they would ask me to draw God, I would draw my grandmother smiling. I would draw... [her] with her hands open, as if to say, 'Come with me because I am waiting for you.' God is strength for the *lucha* [struggle], strength to keep going, to encourage."

Jesus' Parents

Think about the life of Jesus. What did he learn from his mother and father? Surely Mary taught him about courage: his journey to Calvary and through the teeth of death could not have been undertaken without a mother's support. She shared with him her habit of reflection: "Mary treasured all these words and pondered them in her heart" (Luke 2:19). Watching her knead dough gave him a key image for the kingdom of heaven, and her prompting led to the first miracle at Cana.

Joseph must have taught him how to trust the individuals we love, even in the face of social disapproval and legal sanctions. He was a man who believed his dreams, even when they sent him off on inconvenient trips to Egypt with a new baby in tow. Jesus may have remembered Joseph's lathes and wood chips when he asked the women on the way to Calvary: "For if they do this when the wood is green, what will happen when it is dry?" (Luke 23:31)

God's Presence in Your Life

Recall a time during the last week when you felt the presence of God. This does not necessarily have to be a bolt-of-lightning, dramatic event, or something you experienced in church. It is more likely to be an experience of God in the ordinary: a deep conversation with a friend, a glimpse of an apricot-colored sunrise, a cup of hot coffee on a cold morning, a child's hair glistening in the sunlight, a snatch of lovely music.

How do you experience God now? _____

_____

_____

_____

You may want to reach deeper into memory and describe your experience of God when you were a child. For instance, some may recall grandma's singing in the garden while she watered roses around the statue of St. Francis.

How did you experience God as a child?_____

_____

_____

_____

_____

Here's an example from Anne Tyler's novel, *Dinner at the Homesick Restaurant*. Shortly before her death, Pearl Tull finds a diary entry from her childhood: "Early this morning I went out behind the house to weed. Was kneeling in the dirt by the stable with my pinafore a mess and perspiration rolling down my back, wiped my face on my sleeve, reached for the trowel, and all at once thought, Why, I believe that at just this moment I am absolutely happy.

"The Bedloe girl's piano scales were floating out her window and a bottle fly was buzzing in the grass, and I saw that I was kneeling on such a beautiful green little planet. I don't care what else might come about, I have had this moment. It belongs to me."

Faith Sharing
Andrew Greeley reports that 39 percent of adults responding to a national survey had had a mystical experience (that is, a strong sense of God's presence), but 50 percent of these people had never mentioned it to anyone.

How do you feel about sharing such an experience?_____

_____

_____

How would you encourage another person to share such an experience?

_____

_____

_____

Formal Religious Education
Spend some time remembering your own formal religious training.

What were its positive aspects? _____

_____

_____

What would you prefer not to pass on? _____

_____

_____

What role did informal religious experiences (such as those above) have

in your early faith development?_____

_____

_____

Images of God
Describe your image of God:

at age 5_____

_____

_____

at age 15 _____

_____

_____

at present _____

_____

_____

What image of God would you like to convey to a young person? How

would you do so?_____

_____

_____

Anger at God

Keep in mind that our relationships with God are not always rosy. Scripture records many examples of people arguing with God—and God doesn't always win. For instance, Abraham bargained with God to preserve a few good people in Sodom (Genesis 18:16-33). Jacob wrestled with God, and despite a wrenched hip sputtered, "I will not let you go, unless you bless me" (Genesis 32:22-32).

The following questions could uncover some pain, but tough issues are important to consider. As we sponsor or parent children, we do so with the humility of "wounded healers," knowing we're not perfect, yet being willing to let even our scars help.

Have I ever felt angry at God? Can I tell God about it?_____

_____

_____

Does some area of my past need healing? What can I tell God about it?

_____

_____

_____

How might my experience of surviving hurt be helpful to a child? _____

_____

_____

Inviting Questions

In the precatechumenate period especially, the model of the initiating church is a big ear, reverently inclined toward the child. This is the time to invite children's questions, but it may take some skill to draw them out.

Keep in mind that children may also take a tangent rather than ask directly. The child who comments that other children's pictures in school are all terrible is in fact asking, "What happens here if I paint an ugly picture?" The child who seems morbidly curious about a dead squirrel may actually seek an understanding of other deaths or losses, but it's easier to talk about the squirrel than about a relative who died.

Ask yourself:
- What story from my own life experience might relate in some way to the child's question?
- What in my faith tradition has been a resource when I have confronted questions like this?

Tapping Life Experience

Here's how one mom handled the disappointment of a fourteen-year-old son, who didn't get the scholarship he'd wanted from an expensive private high school. He complained that all his work on grades and extracurricular activities had been futile; he worried that his parents wouldn't be able to afford the tuition.

Together, mom and son went for a walk. She listened to his concerns, then told about a time she hadn't gotten the college scholarship she had wanted. That refusal had prompted her to attend another college, which in the long run turned out to be the better choice. "Sometimes a 'no' turns into a 'yes,'" she concluded. "The final word isn't in yet."

Four years later, as president of the senior class, her son led the procession into high school graduation. The master of ceremonies, he led the graduates in a round of applause for their parents. His eyes met hers above five hundred heads, and she wondered if he remembered that day of disappointment, their talk and her encouragement not to give up yet.

Tapping Faith Tradition

A father and daughter struggled together with the question, "Why did grandma have to die?" After they shared their fondest memories of her, laughed at her jokes and cried because they missed her so much, the dad explained that what helped him were Jesus' words: "Those who believe in me, even though they die, will live" (John 11:25).

"Because I believe in Jesus' resurrection, I know I'll see her again," he told his daughter. "And because you have the same color eyes as grandma did, I think of her when I see you. Because she lives on in us, she will never die." During their time of grieving, he also shared with his daughter some of the near-death experiences he'd read about. The people who told these stories had experienced a profound peace and a beautiful light as they came near death. That reassurance helped ease some of his sorrow and fear.

Chuckling at Ourselves

In a lighter vein, we can remember Kevin if we take our role too seriously. Dawdling over breakfast one morning, he asked his mom, "Do you like the pope?" Carefully choosing her words, she explained that the pope had done many fine things, but that she didn't personally agree with everything he said. Although she was in a hurry to get to work, she tried to nuance her position as carefully as possible, then leave the door open for Kevin to respond. He looked at her puzzled as he replied, "I don't like the pope in my orange juice." After all that, Kevin had been asking his mom's opinion of *pulp*.

Chapter 5

A Wondrous Cupboard: Children's Spirituality

Richard Rohr tells the story of the four-year-old anxious to be alone with his newborn brother. After he had shooed his parents out of the nursery, he bent over the crib and whispered to the baby, "Quick! Tell me where you came from. I'm beginning to forget already."

Extensive research in recent years confirms what those who know children have long suspected. Beneath their often grubby exteriors, children know things about God that no one has told them. Under the T-shirt stained with grape juice, they carry a deep yearning for God and cherish a special union with God. Their sense of wonder, total presence to the moment and spontaneity are natural gifts that adult contemplatives work hard to achieve.

Expressing Spirituality

Do not expect children to spout theology. Their images and ideas of God are anchored in practical, concrete experience. Their intuitions are not necessarily expressed in religious language, but in art, gesture, story, silence and innovative speech. Two examples may indicate what to look for in the realm of children's spirituality. Asked to complete the sentence "I saw God in...," nine-year-old Margaret wrote in her journal along with vivid crayon cartoons:

- "I saw God in my friend Jennell because when I broke her ruler she didn't get mad. She just laughed and said, 'oops.' P.S. I didn't do it on purpose."
- "I saw God when we visited my mom's aunt and uncle in St. Louis. All these people came together and they had a lot of food! It must have taken a while to cook all this, but they did all of it just for us!"

Completing the sentence, "I can bring the light of Jesus to others by...," Felipe may not use churchy language, but he offers concrete, practical suggestions: "helping people in a subject they're not very good at, feeding their pets when they are away on a trip, acting real happy even when I wanted a different gift than I got."

Although they may give few external indications, children have thought long and hard about who God is. For this reason, the precatechumenate is a time for listening rather than for lecturing. We can learn from children more than we can teach—if we hear them and refrain from imposing our preconceived notions. It is difficult to summarize all the research on children's spirituality, but from it have emerged some ideas that particularly enrich the initiation process:

- Children's spirituality does not necessarily spring from their environment. In other words, the child of atheists can have more profound insights on God than the child of practicing Catholics.
- Children's notions of God are moored in the particular. They come directly from everyday life. To children, heaven and hell aren't pie-in-the-sky; they happen right here and now.
- Children's deep needs are met by God's infinite love. This does not mean that religion substitutes for what some children lack (for example, adequate parenting). It does mean that even children who have had dismal experiences aren't doomed. The adult may face what Sofia Cavalletti calls "a mouth opened wide in eagerness." Faith assures us that God has many faces, many mansions. With great joy, we can then serve as a channel between God's love and the children's longing.
- Children's quest for meaning is essential to human nature. C. Madelaine Dixon wrote: "Each child must plumb vastness and infinity. Let him [her] call it what he [or she] will—fire, water, death, God, worlds, stars. And somehow he must share his curiosity and his awe before he has formed many static answers...We forget that the probing of strange phenomena, creation, God, death, magic, has made our scientists, our artists, our religious leaders, throughout the ages. Why should we shorten this probing or cover it up for children?" (Quoted in *Children's God* by David Heller, p. 10.)

Affirming Spirituality

Knowing all this, what do we do about it?
- Affirm the child's questions, probings and wonderings, even if they

A Practical Guide to the Precatechumenate

come at odd times or in unfamiliar language. For instance, Zach was shocked after he heard the story of Jesus' crucifixion for the first time. Puzzled, he asked, "then why do you call it *Good* Friday?" His catechist affirmed his question by saying, "the famous poet T.S. Eliot asked the same thing. He said, 'in spite of that, we call this Friday good.'"

- Try to discern what face of God the child most needs. Later in this chapter we explore various images of God. Which one speaks most directly to the child in your care? All Christians, children included, answer in their lives Jesus' question to the disciples: "Who do you say that I am?" (Mark 8:29) Rephrase this for a child: Who is Jesus for you? (A family might brainstorm all they know about Jesus, and all they wonder about him.)

- Create opportunities to attend to God's presence in our lives. A child may learn more about God from looking at a starry sky than from a whole homily on creation.

- Bring faith into the most ordinary routines.

In the Celtic tradition, every household chore (washing the face, making the bed, brewing the beer) was done with a prayer that gave it meaning. People even asked the saints to twine their arms around the cows! In this way, they consecrated every minute to God and lived assured that they were always in God's hands. Conveying that attitude to our children can give them a deep security and confidence.

- Celebrate the wonderful variety of feasts and fasts, seasons and cycles in the church year. Children are more drawn to everyday celebrations at home than to formal liturgies at church because they can participate more directly and aren't staring at the backs of heads. Simple observances of Advent and Lent, Epiphany, Pentecost, birthdays and saints' feasts can be concrete and experiential. Rather than prompting another outpouring of words, they can engage all the child's senses with their particular songs, textures, movements, tastes and smells.

As we try to seize the opportunities suggested by the child, poet Mary Oliver offers good advice: "To pay attention, this is our endless and proper work." The focus of the precatechumenate is on the issues that fill the child's life. As we listen to these, we may be delighted, surprised or shocked. But what we hear now and respond to sensitively forms the basis for the rest of the initiation process.

Exploring the Cupboard of Spirituality

The following approach may help to explore the child's concerns and interests. Adapt it for the children you companion: some will be more comfortable with small group discussion, others with one-on-one interaction, some with writing or drawing their response.

Finding God in Everyday Life
(*adapted with the permission of the North American Forum on the Catechumenate*)

Ask the child:
When was the last time...
- you found a new friend?
- you cried?
- someone forgave you?
- you forgave someone?
- a baby was born in your family?
- you saw something beautiful in nature?
- you felt sad?
- you were sick or frightened?
- you felt like singing, dancing or jumping for joy?
- someone close to you died or moved away?

Choose one of these events (or more if you can extend this over a period of time). Tell the story of what happened. It may be easier for the child to tell the story after you model telling one of your own. "Break open" or explore the meaning of the event by considering:
- how did you feel before this happened? while it was happening? after it happened?
- did you have any questions about it then? now?
- what people were there with you?
- did this event change you? If so, how?
- what *one* word best describes this event?
- would you like to make a picture of it? mime it? dance it?
- how do you think God was present in this event?

If the last question seems heavy-handed, approach it more creatively. One catechist dressed as Sherlock Holmes, with tweed cape and pipe, asked children, "Where can I find God?" They mentioned the Bible and the Mass, then with a little prompting, gleefully pointed to each other.

Images of God

Our images of God are more important than our ideas of God because they are rooted at such a deep level of our psyches. Paul Philibert proposes that we landscape the religious imagination of the child. We do so by providing abundant images of God and of God's reign.

Think, for example, how Jesus drew on images from his childhood to describe the reign of God. Salt and leaven, lost coins and sheep, stories and meals, birds and flowers were household fixtures that he invested with new meaning.

Continuing his tradition, the saints and poets have found that childhood images can become channels of grace throughout life. For example, St. Ignatius Loyola once counseled a young priest who was depressed. He did not lead him through the *Spiritual Exercises*; instead, he roasted chestnuts and did Basque dances from the man's childhood. Recalling, through sense appeal, the memories of a happier time had the desired effect: restoring the priest's good humor.

Some children have a punitive image of God: this angry figure hovers over them, waiting to punish the slightest misdeed. Other children may not have such an extreme idea of God, but their concept may be narrow: the old man with the white beard, for instance. Most children will benefit from introduction to a wide variety of images. Then they can select from this "cupboard" the ones that resonate most deeply for them personally.

To use the following set, you might ask, "If God were an eagle, what would God do? How would God look? Do you want to draw a picture of that eagle, or act out its flight?"
- eagle (Deuteronomy 32:11-12)
- lion or leopard (Hosea 13:7)
- mother bear (Hosea 13:8)
- rock (Psalm 62:2)
- hostess (Proverbs 9:1-6)
- fortress (Psalm 59:17)
- laundress (Isaiah 4:4; Psalm 51:7)
- tower (Psalm 61:3)
- vine (John 15:1-8)
- mother hen (Matthew 23:37)

- bread (John 6:48-51)
- light (John 8:12)
- shepherd (John 10:1-18)
- water (Psalm 63:1; John 7:37-38)
- potter (Isaiah 64:8)
- friend (John 15:13-16)

Play as Prayer

"Play is a child's prayer," writes Jean Fitzpatrick. To understand prayer with children may require us to broaden our concept of prayer. Perhaps prayer for a child could include a perfectly pitched baseball, a humming-bird in flight, the first tulip poking out of muddy ground, a sloppy kiss. The child's joy in the everyday miracle praises God.

Scripture gives us examples of play as prayer. Perhaps the most memorable are David dancing before the ark and Miriam playing her tambourine on the shores of the Red Sea. Creation is seen as play; Wisdom says, "I was his delight, playing before him always, rejoicing in his inhabited world and delighting in the human race" (Proverbs 8:30-31).

Through play, children are also integrating faith, forming a relationship with God that is more than intellectual. If we present them only with doctrine that is codified and set in stone, they can respond only one way: by learning it. If, however, we invite them to playfully enter the mystery, they can bring to faith their gifts of imagination, creativity and sensitivity.

Experiential Approach

The research on children's spirituality confirms what common sense would tell us: the best approach to children's learning is rich in sense appeal. "Hands-on learning" is popular now, and it's easy to see why. Children enduring long, abstract lectures squirm and eventually act out their boredom. Children creating a project are absorbed in their task. As the Chinese proverb says,

I hear and I forget.
I see and I remember.
I do and I understand.

Elizabeth was a bright child who finished her worksheet on the Trinity quickly. Then she politely asked her catechist where she could throw it away. She didn't dream of trashing the pretzel she had carefully kneaded, shaped and baked to symbolize the arms folded in prayer. She devoured it happily when it emerged, hot and fragrant, from the oven.

In this regard, children are not so different from adults. We cherish the Catholic tradition not only for its teachings, but also for its "smells and bells." We believe that everything has the potential to be a sacrament of God's presence, because without God's life within, nothing would exist. As Jim Dunning says, Christians see the world as "brimming with sacraments, icons and images of God."

If we help children recognize God in their experiences, we lead them to the insight of Thomas Merton: "It is God's love that warms me in the sun and God's love that sends the cold rain. It is God's love that feeds me in the bread I eat...It is God who breathes on me with light winds off the river and in the breezes out of the wood."

Chapter
6

Prayer and Ritual in the Precatechumenate
Prayer

Mention prayer at home, and some people get the jitters. For centuries, Catholics relied on priests and religious to lead them in prayer. Now that we are bringing prayer into our homes and assuming our rightful roles as leaders of the domestic church, we may at first feel awkward. This chapter has "tips for the transition." Praying with children may still feel uncomfortable at first. But as with tennis, crafts or cooking, the more we do it, the better we get. Remember too that children readily forgive adult bumbling and sometimes, mercifully, take the lead in prayer themselves.

Informal Prayer

The *Rite* directs that prayer during this period should be informal. That's good news for those who may feel uncomfortable about participating in formal public rites: we have time to work up to them. For now we can follow the KISS rule: Keep It Short and Simple. We also have a rare opportunity to introduce children to a whole variety of informal prayer forms. From this "smorgasbord," they can then select the style that best suits them. The underlying hope is that they will also make prayer and reflection a constant in their lives, a habitual turning to God. For children, prayer can mean many things:

> I didn't know...
> ...that looking could be prayer.
> ...that listening could be prayer.
> ...that moving could be prayer.
> ...that singing could be prayer.
> ...that daydreaming could be prayer.
> I didn't know...
> ...that I already knew how to pray.

Five simple ways to pray at home:

- Enlist the children's help in gathering beautiful wood chips, pebbles or shells. Place these in a basket, then gather in a circle. Pass the basket around. As each person takes an object out of the basket, he or she thanks God for some blessing that has come during the day or the week. Then pass the basket back. As family members return the objects, they ask God's help with some problem they will face that day or week.

- Create a litany of names for God. You may write these on a long sheet of newsprint or make a mural illustrating them. During prayer time, each person simply mentions his or her favorite name, then pauses in silence to image that face of God. Here are some names to prompt your own list: shelter, friend, stronghold, breath of life, comforter, creator, holy one, mother hen, lion of Judah, vine, brother, savior, wisdom, teacher, judge, lamb, healer, king, key, light, protector, way, prince of peace.

- Make or buy a family blessing cup. Any vessel will do, but you may want to keep this one special. Before a meal, fill it with juice, milk or some beverage everyone can drink. Then pass it around, each person drinking from the common cup. The person who drinks offers a spontaneous prayer, like this: "Thank God that Carlos passed Algebra!"; "God, be with Aunt Ethel in her grief"; "We praise you, God, for our new baby cousin."

- Learn the Jesus prayer, which many people like to repeat throughout their day. It can become as unconscious as breathing: "Jesus Christ, Son of God, have mercy on me."

- Say "arrow prayers": brief, straight shots to the heart of God. Sometimes we say them without thinking when the gas gauge nears empty or the child's temperature approaches 104 degrees on the thermometer. The wording may be as simple as "God, help me." The attitude instilled in children is that we can always turn to God in any circumstances without elaborate, flowery words.

You may want to purchase or borrow from your parish library a collection of prayers such as *Catholic Household Blessings and Prayers*, Ed Hayes' *Prayers for a Domestic Church,* or *The African Prayer Book,* selected by Desmond Tutu. You will also want to adapt your prayer to the season: perhaps for harvest or Advent. Remember that prayer for children goes better if it includes some movement, music, objects they can touch, taste or smell. Reinforce the key symbols that they will meet throughout the initiation process: water, oil, light, bread and wine.

Praying with Scripture

Encourage the child to place him or herself imaginatively into the story. For instance, when St. Ignatius reflected on the nativity, he thought of himself fixing the hayrack or helping the animals. Encourage the child to help Martha chop vegetables in the kitchen as she prepares for Jesus' arrival. Invite the child to contribute a lunch of bread and fish to Jesus when he needs to feed 5,000 hungry people. The child can help bear the stretcher for the paralytic hoisted through the roof or for the dead son of the widow of Nain. Here's an example:

- Close your eyes.
- As I read this scripture passage, imagine yourself in it. What do you hear? smell? see? taste? touch?
- Read the passage slowly and reflectively from a children's Bible. Pause frequently for moments of silence.
- Afterward, model the approach: "I smell the dust in my nostrils, see the crowds waving branches and throwing their cloaks down. If I stand on tiptoe, I can see Jesus riding on a donkey. People around me are shouting 'Hosanna!'"
- If the child is willing to share his or her impressions, listen gladly. If the child is reluctant, respect his or her privacy. Perhaps the child would rather make a picture of what he or she imagined or act it out.

Whenever possible, incorporate an experience that corresponds to the scripture. For instance, if you read about the wedding feast of Cana, make water jars from clay as you discuss the story. If you are exploring the meaning of eucharist, break bread together. (Frozen bread dough and bread machines can speed up a time-consuming process, while still conveying the essentials.) The idea is to inscribe the message on as many senses as possible.

Prayer of the Season

As we have seen, prayer with children goes better if it is centered in concrete experience. The church calendar provides many opportunities for feasts and fasts, celebrations that enrich the routine and give meaning to every day. In *A Practical Guide to the Catechumenate*, you can find suggestions for Advent, in *A Practical Guide to Purification and Enlightenment*, ideas for Lent and in *A Practical Guide to Mystagogy*, celebrations for the Easter season.

Ritual

Robert Hovda raised questions about liturgy that are relevant to the initiation of children: "Where else in our society are food and drink broken and poured out so that everybody shares and shares alike, and all are thereby divinized alike? Where else do economic czars and beggars get the same treatment? Where else are we all addressed with the proclamation of a word we believe to be God's, not ours, and before which we all stand equal? Where else are we all sprinkled and bowed to and incensed and touched and kissed and treated like *somebody*—all in the same way?" (Catholic Worker meeting, 5/83)

To his questions we might add, "where else are children and adults treated with equal dignity?"

Children have a deep need for roots. They are convinced that anything done once is a tradition. Anyone who's tried to change the words of the bedtime story knows not to tinker with tradition!

Over the centuries, the church has developed ways of communicating that speak more clearly and profoundly than words. Through rituals, we can give children affirmation and meaning. They can hold these gestures in memory long after they have forgotten the words.

But we must make the connections between the ritual and the lived reality. Otherwise, we run the risk of passing on to our children another collection of empty gestures that do not enhance their journey, but just add more irrelevant baggage.

Thus, the eucharist doesn't make much sense if we have not dined together, sharing stories and jokes and bad moods and flops and successes. The paschal mystery of dying and rising that we celebrate in every eucharistic liturgy takes on meaning when we go home and live out the disappointments as well as the joyous surprises. Around our kitchen tables, failure and fruitfulness can sit close enough to pass the potato salad. One child exults in a soccer goal, another frets over a bad grade. One recites her lines in the school play while another scratches a peeling sunburn. We gather all this when we pray, "Father, accept this offering from your whole family...Let it become for us the body and blood of Jesus Christ, your only Son, our Lord."

Ritual Gesture

Throughout the precatechumenate, the child will meet with ritual gestures in the sessions that can be continued at home as family rituals. For instance, lighting a candle on the kitchen table or playing soft background music can create an atmosphere conducive to prayer. Help the child to focus by providing a crucifix, Bible, vase of flowers, plant, or other beautiful object from nature.

Grace before or after Meals

To say a blessing over meals, you may want to:
- say one spontaneously ("Thanks for the good spaghetti!")
- pray the traditional grace before meals ("Bless us, O Lord, in these your gifts which we are about to receive from your bounty, through Christ our Lord. Amen.")
- sing the "Johnny Appleseed" blessing ("Oh, the Lord's been good to me, and so I thank the Lord, for giving me the things I need, the sun, the rain and the apple seed. The Lord's been good to me.")
- simply ask the children, "What shall we thank God for?"

The Rite of Acceptance or Welcome

This first public rite marks the end of the precatechumenate and entrance into the next period, the catechumenate. It is essential not to explain the rite in advance, so that children come to it fresh, experiencing all that it offers without preconceived ideas. However, some preparation is helpful.

Before the Rite

Prepare for the questions the children will be asked. The presider may use a form of this dialogue or similar words that invite the children to reply, "I want to be a friend of Jesus" or "I want to be baptized" (*RCIA* #264).

- *Celebrant*: What do you want to become?
- *Children*: A Christian.
- *Celebrant*: Why do you want to become a Christian?
- *Children*: Because I believe in Christ.

Beforehand, help children to think about their answers and to articulate their hopes. It is better to respond with a few deeply felt words than with long, memorized formulas.

Components of the Rite
Entrance into the Church

This may vary from parish to parish, but the members of the community surround the children and adults to be initiated, welcome them with song and lead them into the church.

Signing with the Cross

The parent or sponsor will make the sign of the cross on the child's forehead, and depending on the parish custom, also on the child's ears, eyes, lips, heart, shoulders, hands and feet.

You might talk with the child about the way a parent will kiss a baby's tiny hands, feet, ears, etc. This ritual is similar, but goes beyond showing affection. It claims the whole person for Christ.

Presentation of the Bible

Depending on the parish, the child may be given a Bible. You may want to write a personal message on the inside cover, telling the child how special he or she is and marking the date of the rite of acceptance or welcome.

During the Rite

The role of the sponsor or parent is to guide the child, perhaps with a hand on the shoulder, through the rite. You are presenting the child to the community and saying that you support him or her on the path to full sacramental initiation. The presider may ask a question like this:

- Are you willing to support this child as he or she prepares for baptism?

After the Rite
Discuss with the child:
- How did you feel about the rite?
  — about standing before the community?
  — about the questions you were asked?
  — about being marked by the cross?
- What part of the rite was your favorite?

Resources for Further Reading

On the Spirituality of Children

Cavalletti, Sofia. *The Religious Potential of the Child*. Chicago: Liturgy Training Publications, 1992.

Coles, Robert. *The Spiritual Life of Children*. Boston: Houghton Mifflin, 1990.

Corkille-Briggs, Dorothy. *Your Child's Self-Esteem*. New York: Doubleday, 1970.

Fitzpatrick, Jean. *Something More: Nurturing Your Child's Spiritual Growth*. New York: Viking, 1991.

Westerhoff, John. *Will Our Children Have Faith?* New York: Seabury Press, 1976.

Family Resources

Catholic Household Blessings and Prayers. Washington: U.S. Catholic Conference, 1988.

Degidio, Sandra. *Enriching Faith Through Family Celebrations*. Mystic, CT: Twenty-Third Publications, 1989.

Ghezzi, Bert. *Keeping Your Kids Catholic*. Ann Arbor, MI: Servant Publications, 1989.

Hayes, Ed. *Prayers for a Domestic Church*. Leavenworth, KS: Forest of Peace, 1989.

Herbert, Christopher. *The Prayer Garden: An Anthology of Children's Prayer*. San Francisco: Harper Collins, 1995.

Thomas, David and Mary Joyce Calnan. *The Catechism of the Catholic Church: Familystyle*. Allen, TX: Tabor Publishing, 1994.

McGinnis, Kathleen and James. *Parenting for Peace and Justice: Ten Years Later*. Maryknoll, NY: Orbis, 1990.

Tutu, Desmond, ed. *The African Prayer Book*. New York: Doubleday, 1995.

On the Rite of Christian Initiation for Children

Bernstein, Eleanor and John Brooks-Leonard, eds. *Children in the Assembly of the Church*. Chicago: Liturgy Training Publications, 1992.

Brown, Kathy and Frank Sokol. *Issues in the Christian Initiation of Children*. Chicago: Liturgy Training Publications, 1989.

International Commission on English in the Liturgy. *Rite of Christian Initiation of Adults*. Study Edition. Collegeville, MN: Order of St. Benedict, 1988.

Kelly, Maureen and Robert Duggan. *The Christian Initiation of Children: Hope for the Future*. Mahwah, NJ: Paulist Press, 1991.

Nathan Mitchell. *Eucharist as Sacrament of Initiation*. Chicago: Liturgy Training Publications, 1994.

Searle, Mark. *The Church Speaks About Sacraments with Children*. Chicago: Liturgy Training Publications, 1990.

Victoria Tufano, ed. *Readings in the Christian Initiation of Children*. Chicago: Liturgy Training Publications, 1994.

On Lectionary-Based Catechesis

DeVillers, Sylvia. *Lectionary-Based Catechesis for Children*. Mahwah, NJ: Paulist Press, 1994.

Dunning, James. *Echoing God's Word*. Arlington, VA: North American Forum, 1993.

Living the Good News Curriculum. Denver, CO: Living the good News, Inc., 1995.

Videotapes

Neumann, Don. *The Catechumenate for Children*. Allen, TX: Tabor Publishing.

Neumann, Don. *This Is the Night*. Chicago: Liturgy Training Publications.

Audio Cassette

Sokol, Frank and Maureen Kelly. *Preparing Children for the Sacraments of Christian Initiation*. Cincinnati, OH: St. Anthony Messenger Press, 1989.